Indian-born DEBJANI CHATTERJEE and Anglo-Irish poet BRIAN D'ARCY are a highly regarded husband and wife team whose work is popular in anthologies for children. After many years teaching and lecturing, they are now full-time writers who have written and edited over 60 books. Debjani's books include *Animal Antics,* created during a writing residency at Sheffield Children's Hospital, the award-winning *The Elephant-Headed God and Other Hindu Tales* and most recently *Monkey King's Party.* An Olympic Torchbearer for the 2012 London Olympics, her many honours include an honorary doctorate and an MBE. Brian enjoys writing funny limericks, sober sonnets and tragic villanelles. His books include *Tha Shein Ukrosh: Indeed the Hunger,* poems about the Irish Famine, and jointly with Debjani, *Let's Celebrate! Festival Poems from Around the World.* They live in Sheffield.

SHIRIN ADL was born in the UK but was brought up in Iran. She studied Illustration at Loughborough University, going on to win the Hallmark M & S Talented Designer Award. She was Booktrust's official illustrator for Children's Book Week in 2010. She is the illustrator of *Ramadan Moon* with Na'ima B Robert, *Let's Celebrate! Festival Poems from Around the World* with Debjani Chatterjee and Brian D'Arcy, *Pea Boy: Stories from Iran* and *Shahnameh, the Persian Book of Kings,* both with Elizabeth Laird. She also wrote *I is for Iran,* with photographs by her husband, Kamyar Adl. Her latest picture book, which she both wrote and illustrated, is *The Book of Dreams.* She lives in Oxford with her husband and young son.

For Karunawathie T M and Namita Bala,
whom it has been a privilege to sponsor through Plan International,
and for their brothers and sisters and all the children in their districts of Badulla,
Sri Lanka, and Dinajpur, Bangladesh – *Aunty Debjani & Uncle Brian*

For my beautiful and glamorous Mamanjoon – *Shirin*

The publishers and editors would like to thank the following for permission to reprint their copyright material:
Susmita Bhattacharya for her translation of Dance, Dance! copyright © 2011 Susmita Bhattacharya; Catherine Benson for The Chinese Dragon copyright © 2000 Catherine Benson, in *Poems about Festivals* ed. A F Peters (Hodder Wayland); Valerie Bloom for Carnival copyright © 2007 Valerie Bloom, in *Celebrate!* (Cambridge University Press); the Estate of RH Blyth for his translation of Under the cherry-blossoms and The cherry-flowers bloom copyright © 1952, in *Haiku* (Hokuseido Press); Mandy Coe for Moon Cakes for Trung Thu copyright © 2001 Mandy Coe, in *Sling a Jammy Doughnut* ed. Joan Poulson (Hodder Wayland); Debjani Chatterjee for Diwali in *Animal Antics* copyright © 2000 Debjani Chatterjee (Pennine Pens), and Colours of Holi, copyright © Debjani Chatterjee 2009, broadcast on BBC CBeebies; Simon Fletcher for Harvest Festival copyright © 2011 Simon Fletcher; Bashabi Fraser for A Card for me Mom copyright © 2003 Bashabi Fraser, in *Rainbow World: Poems from Many Cultures* ed. Debjani Chatterjee & Bashabi Fraser (Hodder Wayland) and On Buddha Purnima copyright © 2011 Bashabi Fraser; Sue Hardy-Dawson for Poe-Tree copyright © 2011 Sue Hardy-Dawson; Estate of Kazi Nazrul Islam for Eid Mubarak! Eid Congratulations!; Wes Magee for Grandma's Easter Eggs copyright © 2003 Wes Magee, in *Read Me First: Poems for Younger Readers for Every Day of the Year* ed. Louise Bolongaro (Macmillan Children's Books); June Masters Bacher for Easter Lily copyright © 2011 June Masters Bacher; Joan Poulson for Harvest copyright © 2009 Joan Poulson, in *A Poem about School for Every Day of the Year* ed. Gaby Morgan (Macmillan Children's Books); Margaret Sayers Peden for extracts from her translation of Ode to Tomatoes copyright © 2000 Margaret Sayers Peden, by Pablo Neruda in *Selected Odes of Pablo Neruda* (University of California Press); Andrea Shavick for Hannukah copyright © 2003 Andrea Shavick, in Louise Bolongaro's *Read Me First: Poems for Younger Readers for Every Day of the Year* (Macmillan Children's Books); Nick Toczek for Tossing Pancakes copyright © 2009 Nick Toczek, in *Number, Number, Cut a Cucumber* (Caboodle Books); Jill Townsend for Hallowe'en copyright © 2000 Jill Townsend, in *Poems about Festivals* ed. Andrew Fusek Peters (Hodder Wayland).
**The editors and publishers apologise to any copyright holders they have been unable to trace,
and would like to hear from them.**

JANETTA OTTER-BARRY BOOKS

First published in Great Britain in 2011 and in the USA in 2012 by
Frances Lincoln Children's Books, 74-77 White Lion Street, London, N1 9PF
www.franceslincoln.com

This paperback edition first published in the UK in 2013

ISBN: 978-1-84780-479-2

Illustrated with watercolour, colour pencil and collage

Printed in China

2 4 6 8 9 7 5 3 1

LET'S CELEBRATE!

Festival Poems from Around the World

EDITED BY

Debjani Chatterjee & Brian D'Arcy

ILLUSTRATED BY

Shirin Adl

F

FRANCES LINCOLN
CHILDREN'S BOOKS

Contents

Introduction

Each day is a special day, a festive day, for some people somewhere in the world. Festivals are mostly happy occasions, adding colour, vibrancy and cheer to our lives. Many mark ancient traditions and events, record history and provide a continuing sense of community. The same festival can have different names in different places, and different customs associated with it.

In compiling this anthology we have not attempted to include poems for every festival as our book would have been impossibly big. Nor do we claim that the poems here are about the most important festivals – every community and culture has its own view of what is important. In putting this book together, we have included a selection of poems that we enjoy and which we hope captures something of the world's diversity. Some of the festivals celebrated in these poems will be familiar to you, while some other festivals and customs may be new.

You may also like to use this set of poems as a starting point to create a collection of your own favourite festival poems. The brief festival notes provided may encourage you to carry out your own further research. Above all, we invite you to enjoy this book and, through it, to celebrate festivals for the very special days that they are.

Debjani Chatterjee   *B D'arcy.*

The Chinese Dragon

I'm the dragon who dances in the street.
I'm the dragon in the festival.
I leap and twist on caterpillar feet.
I'm the dragon who dances in the street.
I snap and snort and stamp to the beat.
I shiver my scales. I can't keep still.
I'm the dragon who dances in the street.
I'm the dragon in the festival.

I'm the dragon of red and green and gold.
I'm King of the Chinese New Year.
I come from the land of stories of old.
I'm the dragon of red and green and gold.
I can breathe out fire or smoke that's cold.
If you've been good then you've nothing to fear
From the dragon of red and green and gold –
The King of the Chinese New Year.

Catherine Benson (UK)

新年快乐

The Pancake

Mix a pancake,
Stir a pancake,
Pop it in the pan.

Fry the pancake,
Toss the pancake,
Catch it if you can.

Christina Rossetti (UK, 1830-1894)

Tossing Pancakes

'All right!' says Dad. 'This should be fun.
Now let me show you how it's done.
Just watch what I do, everyone...'

Now, why've I got this dreadful feeling
Somehow soon we'll all be peeling
Pancakes off the kitchen ceiling?

Nick Toczek (UK)

PANCAKE DAY

Ice Festival

Cool castles and taverns,
Great giants and beasts,
Dark dragons and caverns,
Ice tables for feasts.

Created by hand,
All gleaming and bright;
A snow wonderland
That's floodlit by night.

So get your skates on!
It's the time of year
To join in the fun,
THE ICE FESTIVAL'S HERE!

Brian D'Arcy (Eire & UK)

15

Carnival

Carnival! Carnival! Everybody shout out – Carnival!
Carnival! Carnival! Everybody shout out – Carnival!

Ah walking up de street,
Everybody dat ah meet
Jumpin' up an' shoutin' 'bout Carnival.

Ah climb into de bus,
Everybody meck a fuss,
Jumpin' up an' shoutin' 'bout Carnival.

Carnival! Carnival! Everybody shout out – Carnival!
Carnival! Carnival! Everybody shout out – Carnival!

Ah step into de mall
Everybody start to bawl
Jumpin' up an' shoutin' 'bout Carnival.

Ah drive down to de market
In me car, nowhere to park it.
Dey jumpin' up an' shoutin' 'bout Carnival.

Carnival! Carnival! Everybody shout out – Carnival!
Carnival! Carnival! Everybody shout out – Carnival!

Banner flyin' in de air
An de pickney dem a cheer,
Jumpin' up an' shoutin' 'bout Carnival.

What a party! What a spree!
What a joyful jamboree!
Jumpin' up an' shoutin' 'bout Carnival.

Carnival! Carnival! Everybody shout out – Carnival!
Carnival! Carnival! Everybody shout out – Carnival!

Valerie Bloom (Jamaica & UK)

Three Loud Cheers for Esther

A poem for Purim

Listen to the tale of Esther:
The story of a savvy queen
Who became her people's saviour.
Let's hear: 'three loud cheers for Esther!'

Stamp your feet and shake your gregger,
Drown the name of evil Haman.
Shame on the wicked Minister!
Wipe away his name forever!

For Mordechai let's raise a cheer.
Boost the boos for horrid Haman.
Cheer loud so everyone can hear.
Let's hear: 'three loud cheers for Esther!'

Debjani Chatterjee (India & UK) and Brian D'Arcy (Eire & UK)

19

Saint Patrick's Day

It's
Saint Patrick's Day:
A holy day,
A holiday,
It's time to play,
Hip hip hooray!

March seventeen,
So wear some green.
Put on your smile,
Do it with style
And seize the chance
To sing and dance.

It's
Saint Patrick's Day:
A holy day,
A holiday,
It's time to play,

HIP HIP HOORAY!

Brian D'Arcy (Eire & UK)

20

A Card for me Mom

It is Mother's Day tomorrow
and the shops are full of wonderful things –
candles, picture-frames, pot-pourri in glass dishes,
but I only have money for a card, and there are dozens –
cards with teddies and roses, cards with moms
in dresses, with gold and red hair and blue eyes.
None of them look like me Mom.
If there was just one card to show
Mom with her gold necklace, bangles and earrings,
reminding me of her soft jingle-jangle as she washes
the curry pots or mixes the dough for rotis and nans,
in her silk kameezes and chiffon chunnies – one mom
with long black hair and flashing dark eyes
who looks more like me Mom!

Bashabi Fraser (India & UK)

Colours of Holi

Waters splash!
Colours flash!
Holi's here –
a thrilling time of year!
Red, blue, orange and green,
happy splashes can be seen
on my cheeks and on my clothes,
on my hands and on my nose.
Holi's here –
a thrilling time of year!

Sitars strum,
Tablas drum!
Holi's here –
a thrilling time of year!
Red, blue, orange and green,
sparkling powders can be seen
on the streets and marketplace,
in my hair and on my face.
Holi's here –
a thrilling time of year!

Debjani Chatterjee (India & UK)

Baisakhi

Crystals of sugar
    swirl
as the sword
    stirs Amrit.

Listening to the tale
of the Five Beloved Ones,

who dodged death
by giving their lives
to God.

Anonymous (India)

Cherry Blossom Haiku

The stream in the valley;
Stones too sing songs
Under the cherry blossoms.

Uejima Onitsura (Japan, 1660-1738)
Translator unknown

Under the cherry-blossoms
None are
Utter strangers.

Kobayashi Issa (Japan, 1763-1827)
Translated from Japanese by R H Blyth
(UK & Japan, 1898-1964)

24

The cherry-flowers bloom;

We gaze at them;

They fall, and...

Uejima Onitsura (Japan, 1660-1738)
*Translated from Japanese by R H Blyth
(UK & Japan, 1898-1964)*

Easter Lily

On Easter Day the lilies bloom,
Triumphant, risen from their tomb;
Their bulbs have undergone rebirth,
Born from the silence of the earth
Symbolically, to tell all men
That Christ, the Savior, lives again.
The angels, pure and white as they,
Have come and rolled the stone away
And with the lifting of the stone,
The shadow of the cross is gone!

June Masters Bacher (USA)

Grandma's Easter Eggs

"At Eastertime," Gran said to me,
"it was our special thrill
to paint a dozen hard-boiled eggs
and roll them down a hill.
Down the grassy slope we ran
as fast as we could go,
but we never ever caught those eggs
so very long ago," – SIGH –
"so very long ago …"

Wes Magee (UK)

Dance, Dance
A poem for Rangali Bihu

The boy - Dance, dance, O Sarumai,
Dance, swaying your waist!
The girl -The way you play your dhol,
How can I stop myself from dancing?
The boy - Dance, dance, O Majumai,
Flying just like a butterfly!
The girl -The way you play your pnepa,
How can I stop myself from dancing?
The boy - Dance, dance, O Chenimai,
Dance just like a deer!
The girl - The way you play dhol and pnepa,
How can I stop myself from dancing?
The boy - Dance, dance, O Dangarmai,
Dance, swinging your hair-knot!
The girl - Answering the call of Bohag Bihu,
I came away, throwing my tools!
The boy - Dance, dance, dance,
O Sarumai, O Chenimai.
If you feel hot, I will fan you.

Anonymous (India)
Translated from Assamese by Susmita Bhattacharya (India)

28

Poe-Tree for Arbor day

The Poe-tree
is perfect, the Poe-tree is likeable,
it doesn't need sunlight and it's totally
recyclable. You can cut it into pieces
and stick it back together. It isn't spoiled
by acid rain or washed away by rivers. It's
a shame about those other trees, I was so
very fond of them. I'm bound
to miss green leaves and all their
oxygen. Yes, we do need real trees. Trees
could save the Earth, for our
children's children,
for insects,
beasts and
birds. But
Poe-trees
are easier.
Poe-trees
are likeable;
they don't
need sunlight and
they're totally recyclable.

Sue Hardy-Dawson (UK)

On Buddha Purnima

A hundred brass lamps shimmer
A hundred wick flames glimmer
The golden face of Buddha glows
His legs folded, his eyes closed
One hand raised to bless us all
The monk's bell tinkles in the hall
The incense smoke rises in curls
The full moon shines down on the world.

Bashabi Fraser (India & UK)

Ode to Tomatoes

(Extracts)

The street
filled with tomatoes
midday,
summer,
light is
halved
like
a
tomato,
its juice
runs
through the streets . . .
populates the salads
of Chile,
happily, it is wed
to the clear onion,
and to celebrate the union
we
pour
oil,
essential
child of the olive . . .

it is the wedding
of the day,
parsley
hoists
its flag,
potatoes
bubble vigorously,
the aroma
of the roast
knocks
at the door,
it's time!
Come on!
And, on
the table, at the midpoint
of summer,
the tomato,
star of earth . . .
the tomato offers
its gift
of fiery color
and cool completeness.

Pablo Neruda (Chile, 1904 – 1973).
Translated from Spanish by
Margaret Sayers Peden (USA)

33

Harvest

Pumpkin and apple,
potato and plum.
What time of year
does harvest-time come?

Harvest's in autumn –
the time I like best.
Gold and ripe,
fruit-time, *harvest!*

Joan Poulson (UK)

34

Harvest Festival

The bread of the land;

a pot of potatoes
a leafy hand of carrots
late green tomatoes;
the old gold of onions
some shiny courgettes
and baskets of plums;
strings of purple garlic,
a bowl of blackberries,
an orchard of apples;

a goblet of grapes.

Simon Fletcher (UK)

Eid Mubarak! Eid Congratulations!

Eid Mubarak! Eid Congratulations!
Let each home have celebrations.
Friend or foe, stranger or dear one,
Whether near or far away,
I send you greetings on this day.
I give myself to all, with love for everyone.

In zakat charity I offer God this aching heart forever.
Whether beggar or emperor,
Let us sing of His splendour.
I bring a cup of fellow-feeling;
Come, believers, for Iftar dining.
Come together in love and let us share God's blessing.

Kazi Nazrul Islam (Bangladesh & India, 1899-1976)
Translated from Bengali by Debjani Chatterjee (India & UK)

Moon Cakes for Trung Thu

In Vietnam, the moon glowing white
fills the children with great delight.
For an autumn full moon, big and bright,
brings cakes and sweets. *It's Trung Thu Night.*

Drums and cymbals and dancing feet,
star-shaped lanterns lighting the street.
Stalls sell Moon Cakes for us to eat –
fish and flower shapes, sticky and sweet.

Wearing masks, no one knows who is who:
"Who's there?" "It's me!" "Who are you?"
A sky full of stars, full moon shining through:
Hunter's Moon, Harvest Moon, bright Trung Thu.

Mandy Coe (UK)

Hallowe'en

The pumpkin has an orange skin.
When the candle is put in,
its gums show
in the glow
and it gives a silly grin.

Jill Townsend (UK)

Diwali

Diwali lights are twinkling, twinkling
In the sky and in our homes and hearts.
We welcome all with cheery greeting
And sweets and patterned rangoli art.
Lakshmi flies upon her owl tonight;
Incense curls, our future's sparkling bright.

Debjani Chatterjee (India & UK)

Hannukah

Light the candles
Me and you
One, two

Pray for peace
Evermore
Three, four

Hold hands
Hug and kiss
Five, six

Always love
Never hate
Seven, eight.

Andrea Shavick (UK)

Thanksgiving

For each new morning with its light,
For rest and shelter of the night,
For health and food,
For love and friends,
For everything Thy goodness sends.

Ralph Waldo Emerson (USA, 1803-1882)

The Pilgrims Came

The Pilgrims came across the sea,
And never thought of you and me;
And yet it's very strange the way
We think of them Thanksgiving day.

We tell their story, old and true,
Of how they sailed across the blue,
And found a new land to be free
And built their homes quite near the sea.

Every child knows well the tale
Of how they bravely turned the sail
And journeyed many a day and night,
To worship God as they thought right.

Anonymous (USA)

Christmas Bells (extract)

I heard the bells on Christmas Day
Their old familiar carols play,
    And wild and sweet
    The words repeat
Of Peace on earth, Goodwill to men!

And thought how, as the day had come,
The belfries of all Christendom
    Had rolled along
    The unbroken song
Of Peace on earth, Goodwill to men!

Till, ringing, singing on its way
The world revolved from night to day,
    A voice, a chime,
    A chant sublime
Of Peace on earth, Goodwill to men!

Henry Wadsworth Longfellow (USA, 1807-1882)

The Christmas Pudding

Into the basin
put the plums,
stir-about, stir-about,
    stir-about!

Next the good
white flour comes,
stir-about, stir-about,
    stir-about!

Sugar and peel
and eggs and spice,
stir-about, stir-about,
    stir-about!

Mix them and fix them
and cook them twice,
stir-about, stir-about,
    stir-about!

Anonymous (UK)

THE CHRISTMAS PUDDING

Into the basin
put the plums,
Stir-about, stir-about,
stir-about!

Next the good
white flour comes,
Stir-about, stir-about,
stir-about!

Sugar and peel
and eggs and spice,
Stir-about, stir-about,
stir-about!

Mix them and fix them
and cook them twice,
Stir-about, stir-about,
stir-about!

47

SUGAR

Kwanzaa

Kwanzaa comes along
Just one time a year,
We're so happy it's come.
Weave a m'keka,
Let's drink from the kikumbé,
Zawadi for everyone.
Celebrate for seven days,
Light the Kinara,
Let's let the holiday shine,
Let's all get the Kwanzaa spirit
And we'll have a real good time.

Anonymous (USA)

48

About the Festivals

Chinese New Year is an ancient spring festival when new clothes are worn, lucky red decorations are hung in homes, and there are dragon dances and fireworks. Before the festival, houses are cleaned and business accounts and debts are settled. People gather in family groups, feast, visit friends, and exchange gifts and lucky money. It is a time to remember ancestors.

On **Pancake Day**, also called Shrove Tuesday, people eat pancakes, traditionally with sugar and lemon. It is customary to turn the pancakes by tossing them in the pan. It falls on a Tuesday between 3rd February and 9th March, the day before Lent, a Christian festival of 40 days of fasting and prayer leading up to Easter Sunday. In some places people run in Pancake Races, flipping and catching their pancake while running. In France and the USA Pancake Day is called Mardi Gras. In some countries it is 'Fat Tuesday'. In Iceland it is 'Bursting Day'.

Ice Festivals are celebrated in many lands, the biggest being in Canada, the USA, Norway, China, Japan and Russia. Ice sculptors create spectacular works, including animals, humans, trees and buildings; sometimes using dyes, particularly for competitions. Some Ice Festivals have ice hotels. An ice sculpture's 'life-span' depends on the temperature of its surroundings and ranges from a few minutes to several months. In Canada, with its strong tradition of ice carving, the festival is part of a Winter Carnival. Alaska's festival in February-March includes ice playgrounds. Harbin in China has held an annual International Ice and Snow Sculpture Festival since 1963.

Carnivals are street celebrations held in many cultures around the world and throughout the year. Caribbean Carnival is one of the best known. Trinidad Carnival is the largest in the Caribbean and Notting Hill Carnival in London is Europe's biggest. The 'carne vale' or 'farewell to meat' was originally a party before the Lent fast. Many carnivals are still staged at the start of Lent and culminate on Mardi Gras or Ash Wednesday. Others celebrate the end of cane-cutting, e.g. Crop Over in Barbados and Cuba's Zafra. People dance, sing and parade in costumes. Calypso and steel bands are popular.

Purim is a Jewish festival that celebrates Queen Esther's rescue of the Jews from extinction in 473 BC by Haman, the wicked vizier of the Persian King Ahasuerus. The Book of Esther, known as the Megillah or 'scroll', is read during Purim. Home-made rattles called greggers are shaken to drown out Haman's name whenever it is mentioned. Poppy-seed cakes called hamantaschen or 'Haman's ears' are eaten.

Saint Patrick's Day or St Paddy's Day on 17th March is a feast day to honour St Patrick (c. AD 385-461), Ireland's patron saint, who is said to have converted most of Ireland and parts of Scotland to Christianity. It is celebrated across the world with street parties, parades and, in many towns and cities, green water displays in public fountains. It is a public holiday in Ireland.

Mother's Day, when children honour mothers and give them cards, flowers and gifts, is celebrated on different days in different lands. Also called Mothering Sunday in the UK, it falls on the fourth Sunday of Lent (before Easter Sunday). Lent's fasting is relaxed, so it is also called Refreshment Sunday. Traditionally, Christians visit their nearest large church or Mother Church, a custom called going 'a mothering'. In the USA Mother's Day is on the second Sunday in May.

At **Holi**, a joyous spring Festival of Colours, Hindus throw coloured powders and coloured water at each other as a reminder that Krishna played pranks at Holi. The festival also celebrates the defeat of the demoness Holika. Bonfires are lit and Holika's effigies burnt.

Baisakhi or Vaisakhi is a spring New Year festival for Sikhs. People gather in gurdwaras ('temples') for a continuous reading of the Guru Granth Sahib, for shared meals and celebrations. The gurdwara's flag pole is washed and a new Sikh flag unfurled. At Baisakhi in 1699 Guru Gobind Singh began the Khalsa or Sikh brotherhood when he called for five volunteers to dedicate themselves to God's service. The volunteers were the first to be called 'the Five Beloved'. Most Sikhs are initiated on this day with amrit or sugar-water stirred by a sword.

The Cherry Blossom Festival is a spring festival occurring in different months in different parts of Japan. Thus it is in January in Okinawa and in May in Hokkaido. Cherry blossoms are often illuminated at night. Tea ceremonies, traditional Japanese music and dance take place. Hanami or 'cherry blossom viewing' is essential. In earlier times aristocrats would admire the flowers and write poems. Japan has over 400 cherry blossom varieties. Picnics are held under cherry blossom trees.

Easter is the oldest and most important Christian festival. It celebrates the death and return to life of Jesus Christ. The story of Jesus' last days in Jerusalem includes Maundy Thursday when his Last Supper took place, Good Friday when he was crucified and Easter Sunday when he came back to life. Symbols of fertility and new life such as the Easter egg and the Easter bunny relate to the Anglo-Saxon goddess Eostre after whom the festival is named.

Rangali Bihu, also called Bohag Bihu, is a joyous spring festival of India's Assamese people. During Rangali Bihu young people compose love songs and dance to the beat of the dhol (a kind of drum) and the music of the pnepa (a horn). Traditionally it has been a time to choose one's life-partner. Sarumai, Chenimai, Majumai and Dangarmai are all Assamese girls' names.

Arbor Day ('Tree Day') was first celebrated in Nebraska in April 1872 and is now a festival in all American states. Most celebrate it in April and some combine it with a celebration of Earth Day. National Poetry Day in the USA also falls in April, so Arbor Day also attracts poetry and songs. Arbor Day's ecological message has grown in popularity over the years and American schools in particular celebrate the festival with zeal. Australia too celebrates Arbor Day, while variations of the festival are found in Japan's Greening Week, Israel's New Year's Day of Trees, Korea's Tree-loving Week, Yugoslavia's Reforestation Week, Iceland's Students' Afforestation Day and India's National Festival of Tree Planting.

Buddha Purnima, also called Buddha Jayanti and Vesak, has other names too in various parts of the world. Purnima means 'full moon'. Buddhists celebrate this festival in April or May as the full moon day of Gautama Buddha's birth, enlightenment (nirvana) and passing away (paranirvana). On this day Buddhists particularly engage in charitable work, visit temples, and use flowers, candles and incense sticks in meditation.

La Tomatina is a Spanish food-fight festival, held on the last Wednesday of August in the streets of Bunol near Valencia. This amazing festival began in 1945 and attracts tens of thousands of participants from many countries, as well as all over Spain. More than 150,000 ripe tomatoes are thrown in an hour! Women wear white at this time, while men do not wear shirts. The night before the food-fight, participants compete in a paella cooking competition. Celebrations last a week and include music, dancing, parades and fireworks. The festival honours Bunol's patron saints, St Louis Bertrand and the 'Mother of God of the Defenceless' (the Virgin Mary).

Harvest Festivals the world over are thanksgiving celebrations after harvests. In Britain they have been celebrated since pagan times and are a reminder of an agricultural way of life. Nowadays churches are decorated with baskets of bread, fruit and vegetables. People bring food to a Harvest Festival service and children sometimes bring food to school. It is then distributed to the less fortunate. The festival is held on or near the Sunday of the Harvest full moon, which is closest to the autumn equinox, usually in September. Jews call their Harvest Festival Sukkot or 'Feast of Ingathering' or 'Feast of Tabernacles' and celebrate it at the year's end.

Eid-ul-Fitr or 'the Festival of the Breaking of the Fast' marks the end of Ramadan. Eid means 'happiness'. It is a joyous three-day celebration when Muslims bathe and wear new clothes before assembling at the Mosque. The festival's first night is traditionally spent in meditation and prayer. The Quran was revealed to the Prophet Muhammad during Ramadan, the ninth month of the Islamic calendar, in 610 CE. Muslims fast from dawn to dusk in Ramadan and break their fast with an evening meal called Iftar. They give zakat or alms in charity.

Tet Trung Thu or 'Moon Festival' is an ancient Vietnamese festival to celebrate children and harvests. Held in mid-autumn on the 15th day of the eighth Lunar Month when the moon is at its brightest, parents spend time with children and pass on traditional arts and crafts. Children make colourful lanterns; sing, dance and parade in costumes and moon masks. It is customary to give presents of boxes of sweet moon cakes.

Hallowe'en on 31st October marks the eve of both the Celtic festival of Samhain and the Christian festival of All Saints or All Hallows. The ancient Celts lit bonfires on this night to frighten evil spirits away. It is still considered the one night of the year when ghosts and witches are most active. Hallowe'en activities today include carving jack-o'-lanterns from pumpkins and large turnips, wearing frightening costumes and trick-or-treating.

Diwali or Dipawali, 'the Festival of Lights', is one of the main festivals for Hindus, Sikhs and Jains. It falls on the new moon day between 13th October and 14th November. Oil-filled Diya lamps are lit to symbolise the triumph of light over darkness and of good over evil. Sparklers and incense sticks are lit. Rangoli patterns are drawn at entrances to welcome visitors. Lakshmi, Goddess of Good Fortune, blesses homes where lamps are lit. Hindus say that at Diwali Rama returned to Ayodhya from exile. On this day Jains celebrate Mahavira's attaining nirvana in 527BC and Sikhs celebrate Guru Hargobind's return from prison in 1619.

Hannukah, a Hebrew word for 'dedication', is the Jewish Festival of Lights to symbolise freedom. It marks Judah Maccabee's victory over the Syrians in 165 BCE. The Jews re-dedicated Jerusalem's Holy Temple to God and celebrated the first Hannukah. They lit an oil vessel that should have burnt for one night, but amazingly the oil burnt for eight nights. The miracle is remembered by lighting the Menorah or Hanukkiya, a nine-branch candelabrum. A candle is lit on the first night and on each succeeding night another one is lit, using the servant light on the ninth branch.

Thanksgiving Day in the United States is the fourth Thursday in November. In 1621 the Pilgrims who landed in America held a feast near Plymouth, Massachusetts, to celebrate their first harvest. Turkeys and corn were the main food. George Washington called the anniversary a Thanksgiving Day. In 1863 Abraham Lincoln said it should be a national holiday. Other countries that have their own thanksgiving days include Argentina, Brazil, Canada, Switzerland, Liberia, Korea and Japan.

Christmas is a joyous festival celebrating the birth of Jesus Christ. Most Christian families go to church on this day, and Christmas carols are sung. Turkey or goose, Christmas puddings and mince pies are eaten, and gifts and cards are exchanged.

Kwanzaa is a week-long festival held from 26th December to 1st January. On the last day there is a feast. Kwanza derives from a Kiswahili phrase meaning 'first harvest fruits' but Dr Karenga, who created the African American festival in 1966, added an extra 'a' to the spelling. Participants light black, red and green candles, give gifts and offer libations in honour of African heritage. An *mkeka* or mat, *kinara* or candle-holder, and *mazao* or crops, are among Kwanzaa symbols.

MORE FANTASTIC POETRY ANTHOLOGIES
FROM FRANCES LINCOLN CHILDREN'S BOOKS

LET'S PLAY!
Poems about Sports and Games from Around the World
Edited by Debjani Chatterjee and Brian D'Arcy
Illustrated by Shirin Adl

Thirty-seven poems about thirty different sports and games played all over the world. From football, baseball and cricket to judo and kung fu, from table tennis, netball and cycling to chess, scrabble and swinging – there's a poem and a game for everyone. Find poems about your favourite sports and then discover new ones. The line-up of famous and international poets includes John Masefield, Sir Henry Newbolt, Robert Louis Stevenson, Jack Norworth, Mandy Coe, Grace Nichols, Bashabi Fraser and Muhammad Ali.

A IS AMAZING!
Poems about Feelings
Edited by Wendy Cooling
Illustrated by Piet Grobler

"A delightful anthology exploring feelings and emotions" – *Booktrust*
"A thought-provoking collection with vivid illustrations" – *Julia Eccleshare, Lovereading*

ALL THE WILD WONDERS
Poems about Our Earth
Edited by Wendy Cooling
Illustrated by Piet Grobler

Book of the Month – *Lovereading*
"A rich and original anthology" – *Julia Eccleshare*
"A great selection" – *School Librarian*

Frances Lincoln titles are available from all good bookshops.
You can also buy books and find out more about your favourite titles,
authors and illustrators on our website: www.franceslincoln.com